A Bunkers & Badasses Coloring Adventure

INSIGHT
EDITIONS

SAN RAFAEL · LOS ANGELES · LONDON

TINA: Ha! I knew if I posted about my new campaign enough, SOMEBODY would show up! Welcome, new hero, to the fantasti-magical world that I like to call . . . Tiny Tina's Wonderlands! In this adventure, I'm your tour guide to all kinds of strange and dangerous challenges. Now, is it MY brilliant mind that's filled this land with all sorts of creative characters, peculiar puzzles, lavish locales, and murderific monsters? No doubt, homie. But as the Fatemaker, it's YOUR choice where to go and what to do, so any horrible squishy deaths are on you. Now, let's get going and—

FRETTE: Tina! This is a brand-new player! You can't just throw them in the deep end and expect them to know what they're doing.

VALENTINE: Frette's right! For even the most talented, masterful players started as lowly level-one weaklings desperately in need of guidance.

TINA: But I just want to get to the action . . . we haven't played in weeks! Ugh, Fatemaker, this is Frette and Valentine, they love to BUTT IN with nonsense like logic and reason. Learn to fly by the seat of your pants already, you two! But fine, this being my super-special one-of-a-kind coloring adventure, I GUESS I can explain it a bit, but you better be paying attention!

* **STEP THE FIRST:** Start on Page 1. If that part trips you up, it's going to be a loooong afternoon.

* **STEP THE SECOND:** Read the page. This is where you get to see my storytelling magic in action—you're welcome for that.

* **STEP THE THIRD:** Color the page. My Wonderlands should be a rainbow explosion, so get to scribbling!

* **STEP THE FOURTH:** Choose what page to go to next. Like I said, this adventure is in YOUR hands!

* **STEP THE FIFTH:** Just keep doing that, over and over! You'll hit an ending eventually.

TINA: Now, will it be a good ending? Like I said, that's on you, so don't go blaming me if it's violent and terrible! Also, you better have a d20! This might be a book, but you'll still need to roll for success every now and then.

FRETTE: Tina. New player.

TINA: Agh, fine! If you don't have a d20, you can flip a coin! Or just ignore the roll and choose. Do whatever you want! What'd I tell you about these two, total flow-killers. So maybe they can PIPE DOWN and let us get going. Welcome to the Wonderlands, Fatemaker! Good luck surviving the experience!

TINA: And here comes a brand-new Fatemaker, ready to start the adventure of a lifetime! Ooh, ooh, and now I get to give the speech, everybody shush!

VALENTINE: We weren't even saying anything, we were waiting for you to—

TINA: VALENTINE! SHUSH! Now, a most splendiferacious welcome to our newest, most nondescript Fatemaker!

FRETTE: They wouldn't be nondescript if you gave them time to paint their minifigure first.

TINA: They can paint it on the go, now oh my gee, shush! I'm trying to do the big introduction here! As I was saying, welcome, one and all, to the endless expanses of the Wonderlands! Now refreshed with a whole new slate of awesome adventures, clever characters, and SO. MUCH. LOOT! Come, Fatemaker, and journey forth!

You heard the lady! Journey forth to *Page 3*!

No way you're letting some Bunker Master railroad you! Explore in the opposite direction on *Page 2*.

1

TINA: What? Where are you—there's nothing back there! You're at the start of the adventure, bud, this isn't some tricky trap, those come later. All you find is . . . well, the edge, I'm working with limited table space here.

VALENTINE: I don't like the way that minifigure is looking at us. Those unpainted eyes . . . it's like staring into the infinite void . . .

TINA: Alright, come on, little fella. Turn around, and let's try this again!

Nothing to see here except giants, Ron Rivote. Let's go back to *Page 1* and start anew.

TINA: Awww, yeah! How could you not journey forth? That call to adventure? She's a mighty powerful lady, and nobody can resist her siren song for long. Hark, Fatemaker! As you rush into the unknown, it's not long before you're beset upon by . . . *ahem* beset upon by . . .

VALENTINE: Uh, isn't this usually where something creepy and/or crawly does some besetting?

FRETTE: Yeah, usually something nice and first-level squishy, like a zombie or a cute little mushroom dealie?

TINA: Yes, obviously! I don't . . . why aren't there any . . . where are all the trash mobs I set up?!

VALENTINE: "Trash mob" seems a little harsh. I'm sure those mushroom cuties have feelings.

TINA: Fatemaker! We need to get to Brighthoof and see what's going on A.S.A. possible!

Well, not much to do around here anyway. Onward to Brighthoof by way of *Page 4*!

TINA: You make all the haste to Brighthoof, Fatemaker. As you pass through the city gates, you notice the newly erected statues of Lady Minifred Maxima before hurrying to find . . . wait, who in MY WORLD is Lady Minifred Maxima?!

MINIFRED: Well, you couldn't ask for a better entrance line than that!

TINA: Hey, who the who are you?! I wrote every NPC in the Wonderlands, and I didn't write YOU!

MINIFRED: Well, of course not, Tina, there's nothing non-player about me. Just like this new Fatemaker, I came to play. And thanks to all my hard work, I'm happy to welcome you all to the now evil-free Brighthoof!

TINA: Evil-free? Brighthoof can't be evil-free, are you friggin' kidding me?!

VALENTINE: Ohhhh, like the idea that good and evil have to exist in a state of perpetual counterbalance. Very zen!

TINA: No, like the idea that an evil-free Wonderlands is SUPER BORING! Look how dull and colorless this place has gotten! Fatemaker, I don't know who this weirdo is, but show 'em the business end of your best gun!

You've been waiting three whole pages for this! Take the fight to Minifred on *Page 5*!

Ooh, you know, you really spent more time speccing for the social game. Maybe we can start a healthy dialogue on *Page 10*?

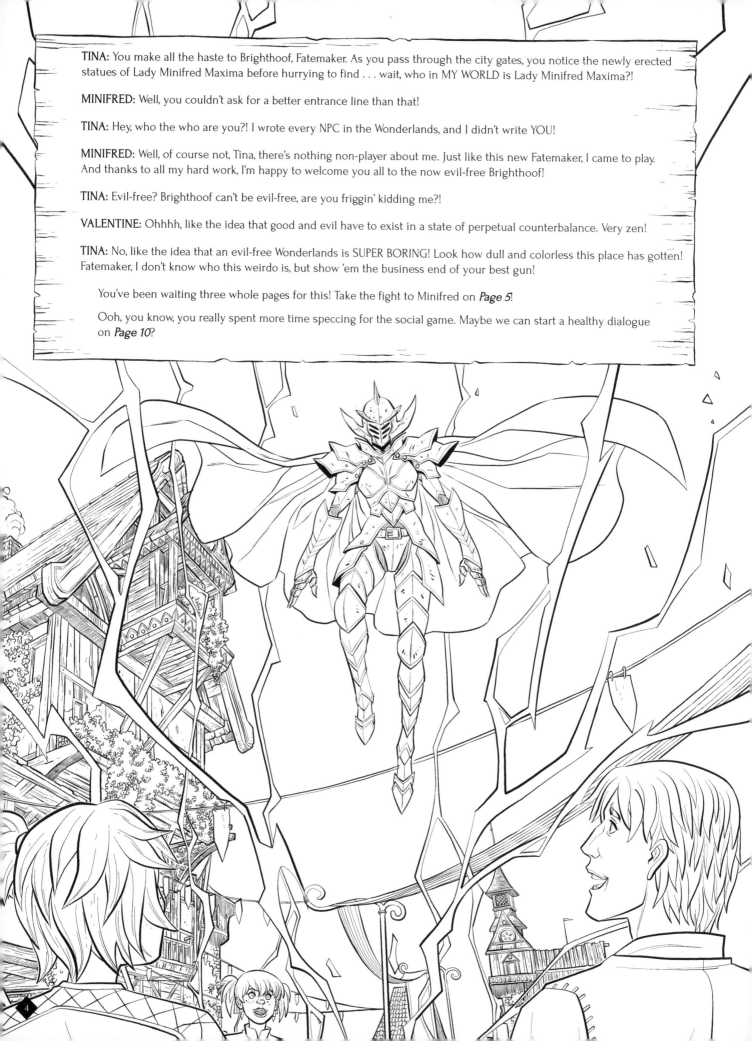

TINA: You take aim and blast Minifred with everything you've got and . . . ohhhh, right, level one, you, uh . . . you don't got much. You don't even have an Action Skill yet. Whatever, you're a Player Character, Fatemaker, I can just give those numbers a liiiiitle bit of a massage, and—

MINIFRED: That wouldn't be very sporting, would it? I followed the rules and leveled up the right way, and so should you! If you were going to have a chance, that is.

TINA: Oh no, she's winding up some real funky spooky magic, Fatemaker. I'm not telling you what to do, but I would GET OUT OF THERE!

Running from the thing that will no doubt killify you is the better part of valor or whatever. Flee to *Page 6*!

She may have high-level loot and strange magics, but, uh . . . well, you've sure got gumption! Take a stand on *Page 9*!

TINA: Some people would call you a coward for running, but I totally get it. You manage to sprint all the way to the city gates and WHERE DID THAT PORTAL COME FROM?! You fall right into the dungeons below Castle Sparklewithers, what? WHAT?!

MINIFRED: I respect that you're smart enough to know when you're beat, but I really can't have you running around out there. You can keep my other prisoner company while I finish cleansing the Wonderlands of evil. Bye-bye, now!

TINA: Dragon Lord? Not you, too! Who is this crazy hottie and what's she done to my beautifully chaotic campaign?

DRAGON LORD: You know, a few weeks ago, I'd have loved seeing you suffer, but now I'm just annoyed. Minifred said I had too big a risk of backsliding into evil to be trusted. Uh, maybe read my backstory, you know? I had a whole redemption arc, thank you very much!

TINA: Yes, and it was heartwarming for everyone involved now TELL US YOU HAVE A WAY OUT OF HERE!

DRAGON LORD: Well, not for myself, but I've got something that might help the Fatemaker. Full disclosure, it could get a bit, uh . . . soul-rending . . .

You signed up to smash skeletons, not have your life essence obliterated. Let's all hunker down and wait for this whole thing to blow over on *Page 7*.

You've only had this soul for like five pages anyway. Take the risk and rend your way to *Page 8*!

TINA: Fatemaker? Fatemaker, are you seriously just going to sit there and do nothing? Where's that sense of adventure I was counting on!

VALENTINE: Yeah, no, they definitely seem to have thrown that right out the window. Or, they would, if this dungeon HAD any windows.

TINA: You see, Frette? This is why you don't invite TOTAL RANDOS you meet on the ECHOnet. You gotta keep those digital and IRL spaces separate!

DRAGON LORD: You know, if you're not leaving, we could play our own game of Bunkers & Badasses. I made these minifigs out of straw, and we could use rocks as dice. Of course, they don't, uh . . . they don't roll too well.

TINA: This! Is! An absolute embarrassment! You don't want to play along? Fine. Time to fall back on old favorites. Meet Miss Sara Lee TNT. ♪She's the Grand Dame of Da-Da-Dayum♪ and she's going to make a DYNAMITE impression on you!

An explosive end, Fatemaker! Maybe roll it back to *Page 1* and make some choices that'll blow Tina away instead of the other way around.

TINA: If your character believes in any higher deities, now might be the time to pray to them. Just sayin', just a thought. Don't even worry 'bout it.

DRAGON LORD: Love the faith you're showing in me, Tina, real great for the still-fragile relationship we've been rebuilding. Alright, Fatemaker, let's see if the little bit of Chaos Chamber magic I've got left can tear open a portal instead of your very being.

TINA: As a Bunker Master with COMPLETE FAITH in her former PC, I'm happy to report that the Dragon Lord's final spell transports you out of the dungeon and to the outskirts of Brighthoof! Minifred is out there somewhere, Fatemaker, so it's time to get you into fighting shape. You know what that means, baby! TIME FOR A TRAINING MONTAGE!

Show the world you've got the eye of the Bullymong on *Page 14*!

TINA: Really? Alright, well, maybe you'll get lucky. You pop in a fresh clip and fire another volley at Minifred and—oh! Oh, she hit you SO HARD! Yeesh, I could feel that one and it's not even my character! Your minifig is flying, RIP. I know she's the villain, but we can agree that was kind of impressive, right? Like, I'm sorry for your loss and all, but you've got to respect, fear, and be a little attracted to that kind of power, y'know?

You are going, going, gone, Fatemaker! Maybe return to the Wonderlands entrance on *Page 1* and try to keep things terrestrial, eh?

TINA: This isn't a side quest, Fatemaker, you can't talk the Big Bad into submission!

MINIFRED: On the contrary, I welcome such a keen mind to the marketplace of ideas. It's quite simple, Fatemaker. I've fully optimized my character to deal with any imaginable scenario. I'm going to solve all of the world's remaining problems, bring eternal peace to the realm, and solve the puzzle that is the Wonderlands once and for all.

PALADIN MIKE: It's right amazin', Fatemaker! Without any threats, we can all take a break, kick back, and enjoy a round at Izzy's Fizzies.

TINA: *Cartoonishly exaggerated gasp* It is one thing to hijack a woman's campaign setting, but now you're putting words in my NPCs' mouths?!

VALENTINE: Didn't you say you got Paladin Mike off the ECHO—

TINA: Fatemaker! Enough talk! Shoot this boombalottie in her stupid gorgeous face!

MINIFRED: Or, counterpoint, you accept the utopian paradise I'm offering and join me. Just a thought.

Mm, it's a mighty fine thought, though, one you can't get out of your head. Head to Izzy's on *Page 13* and chill out.

Wait, why can't you get this thought out of your head? Resist her powers of suggestion by rolling 10 or higher to claw your way to *Page 11*!

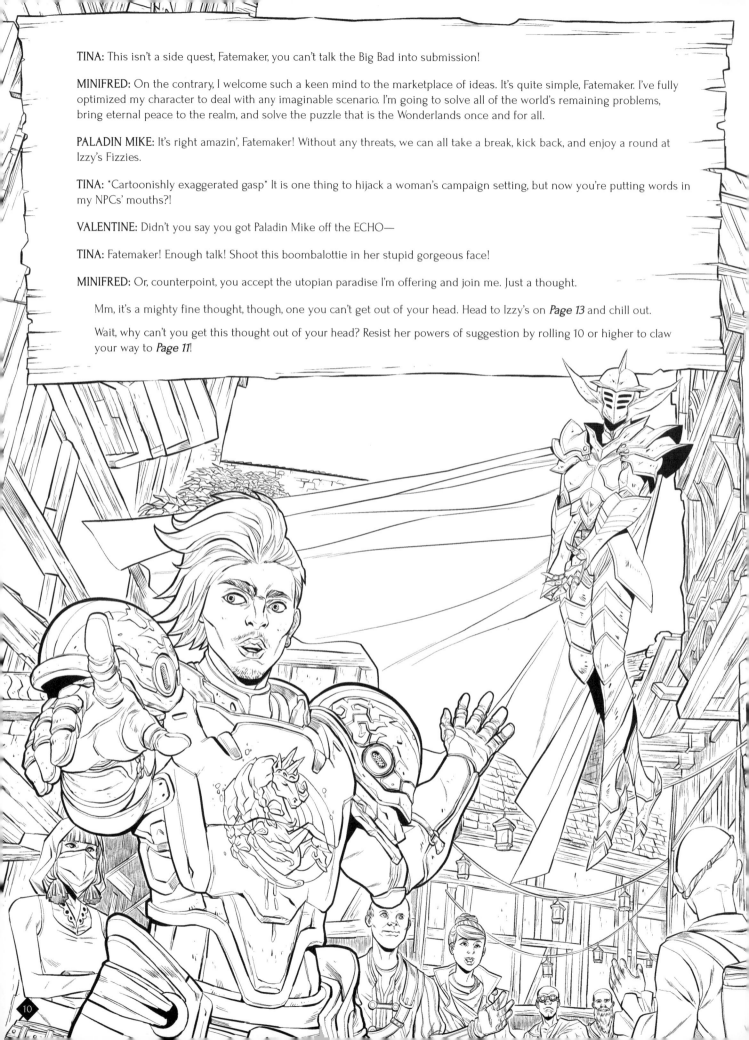

TINA: Wow, you resisted her psychic assault. Look at you and your bad self. I guess mental fortitude isn't just a dump stat after all . . . who knew?

MINIFRED: Very well, Fatemaker. If you will not listen to reason, I will just have to show you. I'll be off to cleanse the lands of evil now. And yes, I can fly after just a few hours of playing, that's how optimal a player I am. Good day to you!

TINA: With that, Minifred flies off, and . . . agh, you have no way to chase after her! Where's a Level 40 character with maxed skill trees when you need 'em? Alright, no time to lose, let's get things in motion!

Uhh . . . well, you don't really have any leads, so just . . . mosey on to *Page 12* to maybe find some?

TINA: Hey! I said motion! Why are you just standing there?

FRETTE: Minifred just flew off, and we don't really have any leads. Usually, you'd give us some kind of clue.

TINA: Wha— I didn't write her, she's a rogue character! What am I going to do, just put words in Paladin Mike's mouth and hope for the best? Hmm . . . eh, actually, I've done more with less.

PALADIN MIKE: Uh, greetings again, adventurer! I was on Minifred's side, but now I've come to my senses and remembered that Tiny is the coolest, smartest, most inventivest Bunker Master imaginable! And because Minifred was in my head, ummm . . . I know that to stop her, you need, uh . . . ooh, ooh! You need to find her character sheets in her secret base and erase her overpowered stats from existence!

VALENTINE: Is any of that accurate?

TINA: So says the most inventivest Bunker Master ever. Paladin Mike's words, not mine. Alright, Fatemaker, time to get you leveled up while I figure out the path forward. Let the trash mobs flow!

Time to show the Wonderlands you're the best around! Don't let anything slow you down on your way to *Page 14*!

TINA: Fatemaker? Fatemaker?! Don't listen to her, she's the enemy!

MINIFRED: How could I be the enemy when we're all having such a nice tea party? You can come, too, Tina!

TINA: Don't you DARE use tea parties for your no-more-evil evil! Fatemaker, adventurers NEED to adventure! You've got to snap out of it. Those crumpets aren't even real . . . listen to me!

Thanks to Minifred, you've found an early retirement! Why even bother going back to *Page 1* to start all this fuss over again?

TINA: As you exit Brighthoof, you find yourself face-to-face . . . to-face-to-face-to-face—okay, there's too many faces to list them all—you see a whole horde of monsters ready to tear you apart!

VALENTINE: Oh yeah, here we go! Now you're in the action, Fatemaker! Nothing like a battle against countless foes to prove your heroic mettle. Will it take ages? Yes. But will the glory you earn be glorious? Maybe!

FRETTE: Yeah, but all these again? Skeletons, mushrooms, goblins? It's all so basic. Can't we zoom through this?

TINA: Hey, these are all classic low-level enemies! You've got to start somewhere!

Valentine and Tina are right. Let's work our way through this with honor and strength on *Page 15*!

You're picking up what Frette is putting down. Let's get Tina to speed up the process on *Page 16*!

TINA: And so, the Fatemaker fought each and every trash mob in their quest to level up. They did so in a completely reasonable time frame, too, FRETTE, because that is the point of a training montage!

VALENTINE: If only we had some triumphant music to underscore this epic battle. I knew I should've brought my boombox this session!

TINA: Finally, as the last skeleton is ground to dust before your mashing melee might, the time has come to head forth and begin the search for the Character Sheets of Minifred Maxima! See, it's all capitalized now, meaning that's an official key item, sucka!

Start looking for that key item on *Page 20*!

TINA: Okay, fine. Fine! You want to do this quick and dirty? Then let's go for quality over quantity. Just going to put this here . . . glue this there . . . come on, get in there already!

FRETTE: Tina, what are you doing with all those minifigs?

TINA: Simple, my dear Frette, I'm making a MAXIFIG! Face the mashed-up might of the gobli-skele-drago-shroom!

FRETTE: Hey, there weren't any dragons on the field before!

TINA: Yeah, but dragon wings make any enemy a buttload-percent cooler! How're you going to take this on, Fatemaker? Show me what you got!

This thing wants to be mashed up? Well, you'll mash it even harder by attacking its body on *Page 17*!

Time to put those social skills to good use! Attack the maxifig monstrosity's mind on *Page 18*!

When all else fails, let love lead the way. Woo this weird warrior's heart on *Page 19*.

TINA: CRASH BANG BOOM, the gobli-skele-drago-shroom swings upon you with its fleshy appendages! Your bullets ping off its spongy, shroomy exterior with no effect!

VALENTINE: Tina, nobody sets such an evocative scene as you do.

TINA: Valentine's attempts at sucking up are as ineffective as the bullets! As the creature bears down on you, you dodge past its blows and . . . what's this? Your melee weapon strikes true and shatters one of the monster's skeletal shins. In retrospect, expecting those bony little legs to carry all that weight was mayhaps too big an ask. The monster collapses, shattering into dozens of defeated goblis, skeles, and shrooms, and one pair of very cool drago wings!

VALENTINE: Did an . . . eraser fall out of that thing, too?

TINA: Yeah, getting all those minifigs to stick together took some work. Fatemaker! Hold on to that eraser for me, will ya? And then get moving—you're leveled up and ready for war!

   You GET AN ERASER and are good to set out to war on *Page 20*!

TINA: You're talking to it? Seriously? It's a big mindless monster and it's trying to kill you, stop trying to find common ground with it!

FRETTE: Actually, as an amalgamation of all those different creatures, this thing has more minds than anything else we've faced before. I think the Fatemaker's appeal to its paradoxical, nightmarish existence is getting through.

TINA: Hey, who's the Bunker Master here? I'll determine what does or doesn't get through to the gobli-skele-drago-shroom. Of course, the sooner we're done here, the sooner we get to stomping Minifred's butt . . . Alright, yeah, your words make this horrifying hive mind aware of its own abominable existence, and it can't help but shudder itself into a full collapse! Bodies rain everywhere! Oh, the horror, the horror!

FRETTE: That seems a little convenient.

TINA: You wanted quick and dirty, you got quick and dirty! Anyway, ding, ding, dingdingdingdingding, oh, look at all those level-ups! Now you're ready to journey forth, Fatemaker. SO GET TO IT!

The level-up dings keep dinging all the way to *Page 20*!

18

TINA: You're talking to it? Seriously? It's . . . oh no, you're not just talking to it, are you? Alright, I see you, Fatemaker, I see you. Speak your heart. Roll that romance check! What'd you get?

VALENTINE: You love to see love bloom on the battlefield!

SUCCESS (10 or higher)

TINA: And bloom it does! The gobli-skele-drago-shroom swoons at your artful advances, Fatemaker, and returns your love the only way it knows how: by absorbing your very being into its horrifying body of bodies. Always room for another minifig in this legion of love!

GLOMP! You are now one with your new love. Go be one with *Page 1* to regain your independence.

FAIL (9 OR LOWER)

TINA: You really do. Unfortunately, that won't be happening today. The gobli-skele-drago-shroom only has one love, and that's crushing the feeble bodies of Fatemakers that step to it. CRUNCH!

VALENTINE: How is this in service to our noble quest?

TINA: It's not, but you've gotta respect the way the dice fall, Valentine, my bud. So I say again, CRUNCH CRUNCH!

CRUNCH! Return to *Page 1* to see about being uncrunched.

TINA: After much journeying, you arrive in the Wasted Wastelands of Wastefulness! You are greeted by your old friend and son-of-a-witch, the Wastard!

WASTARD: Greetings, Fatemaker. You've arrived—

FRETTE: Valentine and I know the Wastard, Tina, but this new Fatemaker hasn't met him yet.

WASTARD: Right. Greetings, new friend! You've arrived—

VALENTINE: Haven't we been here before? This looks a lot like Karnok's Wall.

WASTARD: Indeed, it is. Minifred has drained my home of what little life was left and—

WASTED WASTELANDS OF WASTEFULNESS, HUH?

DON'T YOU MEAN KARNOK'S WALL?

FRETTE: Wasted Wastelands of Wastefulness is a pretty repetitive name for—

TINA: Would you two let me set the scene, gah! GAH! Whatever, Wastard's taking you to the Shadow, he's Minifred's lackey, and he holds the key to her stronghold.

VALENTINE: Tina, we're sorry. We were just engaging in the world!

TINA: It's fine, you're fine. Let's just move on . . .

Maybe take in the scenery and let Tina flesh things out a bit more? Take a minute on *Page 21*.

Get on to facing the Shadow on *Page 22*.

FRETTE: I don't think we can move on until we get that scene setting you were talking about. Right, Valentine?

VALENTINE: Huh? Oh yeah, absolutely not! Wastard, my man! We need you to help paint us a word picture the likes of which my ears have never heard before!

WASTARD: Really? Yeah . . . yeah, okay. So, this place wasn't much to look at before, but now? Sure, the wall was brown, but at least brown is a color, you know? We take the Shadow out, hopefully we can bring some of that vibrancy back, and, uh . . . thanks, you guys. Says me, the Wastard! Not anyone who may or may not be voicing me! This is all in character!

Alright, NOW let's get on to facing the Shadow on *Page 22*!

TINA: You venture deeper into the Wasted Wastelands and find that it's even more of a ghost town than usual.

VALENTINE: For clarity, are we talking metaphorical ghost town, or are there actually ghosts?

TINA: You're going to have to wait and see, my guy. Can't give away any surprises! What you see for sure, though, is a large! Ominous! Horrifying! Awful!

VALENTINE: Oh, here it comes!

TINA: Office building!

VALENTINE: Ahhh! Look out, Fatemaker, it's . . . wait, what?

WASTARD: Yeah, the Shadow built this place for all his nefarious doings. Be careful heading in there, he's got tons of rotten friends. You can go in through the lobby and try to get a meeting or just kick your way in. Your call.

Respect the chain of command and request a meeting on *Page 23.*

Villains don't get to dictate how these things go down! Kick in that door on *Page 24*!

TINA: You make your way into the Shadow's lobby and find a secretary waiting. Her head is slumped, her limbs are stiff, and she has a speaker strapped to her neck. That's right, she's a zombie! See what I did there? He's got ROTTEN friends, heh heh. See what I did there? 'Cause she's the evil kind of rotten, but she's also literally rotting away. 'Cause she's a zombie.

SECRETARY: Greetings there, you big burly adventurer, you! If you're here to see my good friend the Shadow, just go ahead and fill out one of these forms. You can grab it, but don't get too close or I might take a little bite. Tee-hee!

VALENTINE: Is someone voicing that zombie through the speaker? That is deeply upsetting.

TINA: You recover the form and start to fill it out. There are lots of questions about how you'd feel about being the Shadow's friend, or being turned into a zombie, or asking what size neck strap you wear.

VALENTINE: That is also all deeply upsetting.

TINA: You finish filling out the form and the secretary ushers you in to see the big boss himself. And hey, you even pocket the pen you used to fill it out! Who says I don't give you the sick loot?

GET THE PEN and head into your meeting with the Shadow on *Page 25*.

TINA: You're a Fatemaker of action, not paperwork, and I respect that! You storm in past a secretary that looks awfully undead and bitey, kick in the door to the Shadow's office, and find a whole room FULL of people that are undead and bitey! Also, the Shadow himself! He isn't undead, but he fits right in with his chapped lips, cracked skin, and extremely corpse-y vibe.

THE SHADOW: Oh, excuse me, Fatemaker, you caught me right in the middle of a business meeting. My zombie coworkers and I were trying to figure out what to have for lunch, and boy, if they don't always gang up on me and vote for brains. Okay, gang, go on and enjoy, I'm going to have a talk with our new friend here.

TINA: The zombies all shuffle out of the room politely, moaning as they go.

THE SHADOW: You know, as the necromancer who raised them, I could have them eat whatever I want, but as Mama the Shadow always says, that's no way to make friends.

There's a real weird energy in the room, so let's maybe just get to why we're here on *Page 25*.

THE SHADOW: Alright, Fatemaker, I know why you're here. You've no doubt heard just how good I am at making and keeping friends, and you thought to yourself, *Hey, that Shadow guy seems pretty cool, I want to be his friend, too.*

VALENTINE: Ooh, well . . . this is awkward . . .

THE SHADOW: Huh? Oh, you . . . you're here for the key to Minifred's base. Oh, no, no, I, heh, I totally get it, that's . . . and you'll just head off when I give it to you, uh . . . well, I mean, we could still be friends, right? I'd be happy to help my good friend out if you, you know . . . were one. I could even show you the best path to her hiding spot underground in the Table Below. What do ya say?

Yeah, you gotta go with Valentine on this one, this is way too awkward. Maybe just grab that key and skedaddle to *Page 26*.

Better a sad, pathetic friend than a sad, pathetic enemy, right? Hang with your new bud on *Page 27*.

TINA: *THWACK* You hit the Shadow right in his dumb grin, grab the key, and run for the door!

FRETTE: Ha! A classic hit-and-run. Hard to argue with a move like that.

TINA: You would think so, my dear Frette, but all the zombies now swarming into the room actually find it very easy to argue with that move.

THE SHADOW: Okay, that was not a good start, but don't worry! I've met lots of people who were destined to be my friends and just didn't know it yet. In fact, how about a few dozen of those very friends show you the error of your ways!

You punched the Shadow, you can punch all his friends! Fight your way out on *Page 28*.

All these office-working zombies, there's got to be some tension here. Try starting some drama on *Page 29*!

TINA: I don't know if I approve of you hanging out with such shady characters, Fatemaker, but we haven't had an opportunity for a proper tea party this entire game, so I'll allow it. His zombie servants bring you some nice tea, a nice crumpet, one of them gives you a nice shoulder rub—it's all so nice. So nice . . . sooooooo niiiiiiicccccceee.

FRETTE: I do not think her talking like that is a good sign.

VALENTINE: That's way too much nice for Tina, this has got to be a trap! Oh, this is why you don't accept snacks from strangers!

THE SHADOW: Ah, but we're not strangers, Fatemaker. We're the best of friends. Forever and ever and ever and . . . you get the idea, right? Was that enough evers?

You need to roll a 10 or higher to resist this guy's wide, toothy grin and hypnotic voice; run to *Page 30* if you do!

The tea's nice, this place has air-conditioning, and you can get used to the smell of rotting corpses. Chill out on *Page 31*.

TINA: You fight valiantly, Fatemaker, but there's only so much you can accomplish against the unwashed masses that now pile upon you.

THE SHADOW: Just FYI, we'd absolutely have showers, but it is a dickens-and-a-half to get indoor plumbing piped to the desert . . . or to a fantasy world, come to think of it.

TINA: For every zombie you strike down, two more take its place. And eventually, they drive you to the ground, restraining you under the weight of all those rotting limbs.

Well . . . not like you're going anywhere on your own, so let's ask those zombies to drag you over to *Page 32*.

TINA: Fatemaker! What a creative idea! Let's see if it works or if you get eaten by the ravenous undead. You throw your voice, making it sound like one of the zombies is saying, "Uh, before we eat this adventurer, I want to ask Janet why she ate the brains I was saving for an afternoon snack in the break room fridge." The Shadow, eager to have someone play along with his fractured reality, can't help but keep the conversation going.

THE SHADOW: "I've told you, Moriarty, if you don't put a label on it, there's no dibs!" "Everyone saw me put it in there, Janet, and I didn't have a marker." "And who's fault was that?" "You stay out of this, One-Eyed Brian!" "Don't make fun of him, he can't help what body part rotted first!"

TINA: Before you know it, all the zombies have started brawling with each other instead of trying to eat you! And you've already got the key in hand, so . . . maybe, uh . . . you know, not trying to tell you what to do, but . . .

Take the hint and run to *Page 33*, leaving the Wasted Wastelands behind for good!

TINA: With a shake of your head, you manage to overcome the hypnotic suggestions the Shadow is trying to hit you with. In fact, now that you're done with your tea, it's time for you to skedaddle. And surely, you reason, your new bestest bud the Shadow will escort you out?

THE SHADOW: Well . . . a deal's a deal. But you'll come back, right? To see your old buddy the Shadow?

TINA: You reassure him again and again that you'll be back as he escorts you all the way to the edge of the Wasted Wastelands. Goodbye, so long, safe travels, time to head below the surface and find Minifred's secret base.

FRETTE: Don't we want to let the Wastard know we finished our mission?

TINA: Eh, he's a smart boy, he'll figure it out. We've got places to be!

Wave goodbye to the Shadow as you descend into the depths on *Page 33*.

TINA: You slip riiiiiight back in your chair—ooh, so comfy—and listen to the Shadow drone on and on and on. This is the life! Who needs adventuring when you can let a bunch of zombies take care of everything for you? Who needs to worry about the straps being tied around your body? You aren't planning to go anywhere anyway! Yeah, it's just easy-breezy for you, Fatemaker. Don't even give a second thought to that gigantic bone saw the Shadow is pulling out of his desk.

VALENTINE: I don't know, I feel like you really should give it a second thought . . . am I crazy?

Page 32? Yeah, you can go to Page 32, if some of your new undead friends are willing to wheel you there.

THE SHADOW: Don't get me wrong, Fatemaker, it's not that I don't trust our newfound friendship to develop on its own. I've just found it's easier to keep my friends around when said friends are also my undead servants, sworn to serve me until they rot away into dust and ash. You understand.

TINA: And before you know it, it's just a hop, skip, brutal murder, infernal resurrection, and a jump from your new existence as one of the Shadow's undead BFFs. A tragic ending, but hey, newest zombie gets first dibs on brains!

Well, now you've got hundreds of friends, so that's something! None of them are exactly great conversationalists, though, so resurrection is just a quick flip back to *Page 1* away!

TINA: With the key in hand, your journey continues down through a hole in the earth. But it ain't just any hole in the earth, it's a hole into the center of our gaming table!

VALENTINE: Ooh, how meta!

TINA: A meta villain calls for a meta solution! If Minifred wants to hijack my game, then we're going to hijack the playing field and journey into . . . the Table Below! You find yourself in a mysterious realm surrounded by junk food, discarded miniatures, and the very Bunkers & Badasses books that give our world meaning! Anyway, time runs short, Fatemaker! Onward to Minifred!

You've learned your lesson about wandering randomly, so head onward to *Page 34*!

You've learned nothing and you're hungry! Eat those oversized snacks on *Page 35*.

You've learned nothing and you could do with some light reading! Check out all the random sheets of paper scattered across *Page 36*.

TINA: And so, you venture forth, your way lit by all the glow-in-the-dark dice I bought at BunkerCon. Glad to finally have a use for these things! They're cool, but it's not like I'm ever rollin' dem bones in the dark, y'know? They make for great mood lighting, don't ya think?

VALENTINE: I, in fact, do NOT think! The shadows they cast . . . it's like there's something moving in the dark . . .

TINA: Oh, it's not like that at all, V-man, it is PRECISELY that! As you move through the inky darkness, you realize all those old, unpainted minifigs I left in storage? Yeah, they're after you, one hundo percent. In fact, they're coming at you like a tidal wave of unused gray plastic! Seriously, I should not be allowed to spend so much money at BunkerCon!

Alright, you've had mixed success battling hordes so far, but you feel the odds are in your favor on *Page 37*!

You've been bringing color back to the land, why not to these minifigs? Get painting on *Page 46*!

TINA: Oh, Fatemaker, no, those cheese puffs are so old! I can't even remember the last time I had a cheese puff—that one might've come with the table. That wasn't even good for anyone when it was fresh and eaten by someone normal-size. Ooh, yeah, here it comes, that is . . . that is some extreme illness. Yeah, you can't vomit fast enough, you really want that stuff out of you. Wait, ooh . . . ooh, that's too much vomit. Yeah . . . RIP to you, that's death, my dude. Why would you eat that? Terrible idea . . . *CRUNCH MUNCH CRUNCH*

You died as you lived: making terrible choices just to see what would happen. Head back to *Page 1* to start the cycle anew!

TINA: Hey, no, stay out of that, Fatemaker, that is my personal property!

FRETTE: Tina! These printouts are all official errata and updates for the character classes! Why haven't you been keeping us up-to-date on this stuff.

TINA: Ugh, it's all so boring! It's tiny little stat adjustments and tweaks to keep things balanced, it sands all the fun edges away!

FRETTE: Did you consider that these adjustments could help soften Minifred up when we finally face her?

TINA: I . . . of course I did, why else would I lead you this way? Fatemaker, grab as many sheets as you can carry!

GET THE ERRATA SHEETS and continue on to *Page 34*.

TINA: With a swing of your weapon, you cleave through half a dozen minifigs like they're not even there! Bing bang boom, baby, all that training's paid off! I mean, it also helps that none of these minifigs actually have stat blocks, but let's say it was mostly the training! Before you know it, you're the last one standing, surrounded by crushed, flayed, maimed plastic as far as the eye can see. Which . . . again, not very far since everything is lit by dice, but still!

All that combat has left you rather weary. Maybe take a quick rest on *Page 38*.

There's no time to waste if you want to take down Minifred! Continue forth on *Page 39*!

TINA: You made it all the way to our third act before taking your first rest! Normally, I'd explain the mechanics, but instead, a vision appears to you as you drift off. A vision . . . of Minifred!

MINIFRED: Greetings, Fatemaker, I see you're still on about this whole "stop Minifred from saving the world from any and all evil" quest of yours. You do hear how ridiculous that sounds, right? Wouldn't it be so much easier to just let me finish my great work and enjoy eternal peace? I really think you should take this vision as a sign to finally give up. Don't you agree?

You've come too far to give in to Minifred's influence now! Tell her to take a hike on *Page 40*!

You really are quite tired. Maybe go to *Page 41* and let Minifred have this one; she really seems to want it.

TINA: Nothing's stopping you from taking back our game world, Fatemaker, and I respect it! Unfortunately, I only bought so many glow-in-the-dark dice, so the way forward quickly turns dark and dangerous. In fact, you're pretty sure you've seen that six-pack of limited-edition skag-flavored soda before. But what's a little losing your way to an adventurer?

Your misaligned internal compass won't stop you; keep going to *Page 42*! Well, you hope that's where you're heading, anyway.

Alright, maybe you should reconsider that rest on *Page 38* before you get even more lost.

TINA: You give a slight nod to Minifred, doing your best to lull her into a false sense of security. As she nears closer, SURPRISE ATTACK! You bash that game-stealing goober right in her perfect mouth! Oh, the carnage, the destruction, the absolute domination! If only this wasn't a dream and you were actually smashing her face in. Fortunately, her psychic attack lingers even as you wake from your slumber. Her energy is a beacon in the night, leaving you with a mental picture of exactly where to find that busted-build beauty.

It's time to take the fight to Minifred! Follow your psychic connection to her lair on *Page 51*!

TINA: Oh, come on, Fatemaker, you can't possibly—

MINIFRED: That's right, Fatemaker, it's so much easier to give in and let Minifred take care of everything. You don't need to quest, struggle, or worry ever again. In fact, I'd say even waking up would be a waste of your time and energy. Instead, you can drift away into an endless dreamland where you can adventure to your heart's content. Yes, quite good, these imaginings are the only Wonderlands you'll ever need.

And so you drift away into a beautiful dream, never to wake again. If you want, you can even imagine yourself back at the start of your journey on *Page 1*.

TINA: You forge ahead into the darkness, getting more and more lost by the minute. A skitter-scratching noise begins to echo all around you, and the smell of old tacos is heavy in the air.

FRETTE: Cheese puffs and soda are one thing, but if you're leaving whole tacos in here, we really need to have another discussion about basic hygiene.

TINA: Alright, let's put a pin in that to talk about NEVER, because suddenly, a ratch jumps from the shadows to attack!

VALENTINE: Oh, well that's not so bad. Just one ratch?

TINA: Yes, Valentine, just one ratch. One actual-sized, real-world, it's-been-living-in-this-table-eating-old-tacos ratch! The beast towers over your tiny minifig character, Fatemaker, and ooh hoo hoo, it's lookin' mighty hungry.

Nothing! Will! Stop you! Roll a 15 or higher to show this ratch who's boss on *Page 43*! But go to *Page 44* if you fail.

This thing! Will Probably! Stop you! Flee as fast as you can to *Page 45*.

TINA: I'm not gonna lie to you, Fatemaker, this is the greatest challenge you've faced so far, and you needed the best rolls imaginable to take this ridonkulous ratch out. Somehow, though, all your training—you're welcome, by the way—has prepared you well! You dodge the beast's blows, smash up its legs, and break through its hard outer shell.

FRETTE: Carapace.

TINA: *Gesundheit.* And so, with one final blow, the ratch, with a retch, is dispatched! Truly, you are ready for the final challenge ahead. *Sniff* I couldn't be prouder. You catch a glimpse of light in the distance and know, in your heart of hearts, that Minifred Maxima awaits.

It all comes down to this! Make your way to the final confrontation on *Page 51*!

TINA: Gulp!

VALENTINE: Did you just say "Gulp"?

TINA: Yeah, I think a ratch probably gulps when it swallows. I mean, maybe it's more of a gnash or a skronk, but creative liberties! You want 100 percent accurate wildlife noises, go ask Hammerlock. Point is, you're a minifig and it's a full-grown ratch, so . . . yeah, you get eaten right up.

The great thing about minifigs is you can always get a new one. In this case, they're waiting for you back on *Page 1*.

TINA: You make a quick retreat as the ratch gives chase! But you're tired, Fatemaker, and you're lost, and it's dark, and . . . I don't know, some other bad thing, is all that not enough? You put your all into it, barely managing to keep ahead of the ratch's slavering maw. Will you make it? Will you survive? Nope! Instead, blindly running in the dark ends with you running riiiiight over the side of a cliff.

FRETTE: How is there a cliff inside of your gaming table?

TINA: It's actually the hole the ratch used to get into the table in the first place, but you work with what you've got! Should really patch that up. Anyway, you fall to your death! Sorry if I'm underselling your agonizing death.

Technically, you're not dead yet, you haven't hit the *SPLAT*. Oh no, there you go. Hmm . . . back to *Page 1*, then?

TINA: As the wall of minifigs looms, you quickly check your surroundings. Sure enough, you see jars upon jars of acrylic paint. I knew that stuff was in here somewhere, I have GOT to organize this place. Acting fast, you pop the lid off one of the jars, a burst of color sweeping forth! The minifigs freeze, looking at you with a mix of uncertainty . . . and hope.

VALENTINE: Alright, gang, I know what we need to do! Time to paint these rogues rouge!

FRETTE: This is a relaxing way to spend an afternoon. Valentine, can you pass the yellow?

VALENTINE: Which yellow? I've got Terrific Topaz and Honeyed Mustard.

TINA: Over several hours, you carefully bring all the figures back to vibrant life, winning their respect and admiration! So grateful are the multicolored minis, they offer to take you right to Minifred's doorstep!

Trust your newfound friends to guide you to *Page 50*!

This journey is yours and yours alone. Bid your new friends farewell and make your way to *Page 47*.

TINA: As you continue through the treacherous depths of the Table Below, you eventually come across a maiden most fair tinkering away at a rather flingy-looking contraption. This medieval mechanic turns to greet you with a smile as you approach.

LADY ELLE: Well, hey there, adventurer! Fancy meetin' you in a dark, dank place like this. The name's Lady Elle, and I'm a bit of a mover and shaker in these here parts. In that I will move and shake your body wherever it needs to go with my trusty catapult. Somewhere like, oh, say, the fortress of a beautiful, yet scary-beyond-belief rogue Player Character? Any interest in that sort of transport, Fatemaker?

Lady Elle's catapult looks . . . mostly trustworthy. Roll a 10 or higher for a successful trip to *Page 48*.

Should you fail the roll, well . . . let's just see what happens on *Page 49*.

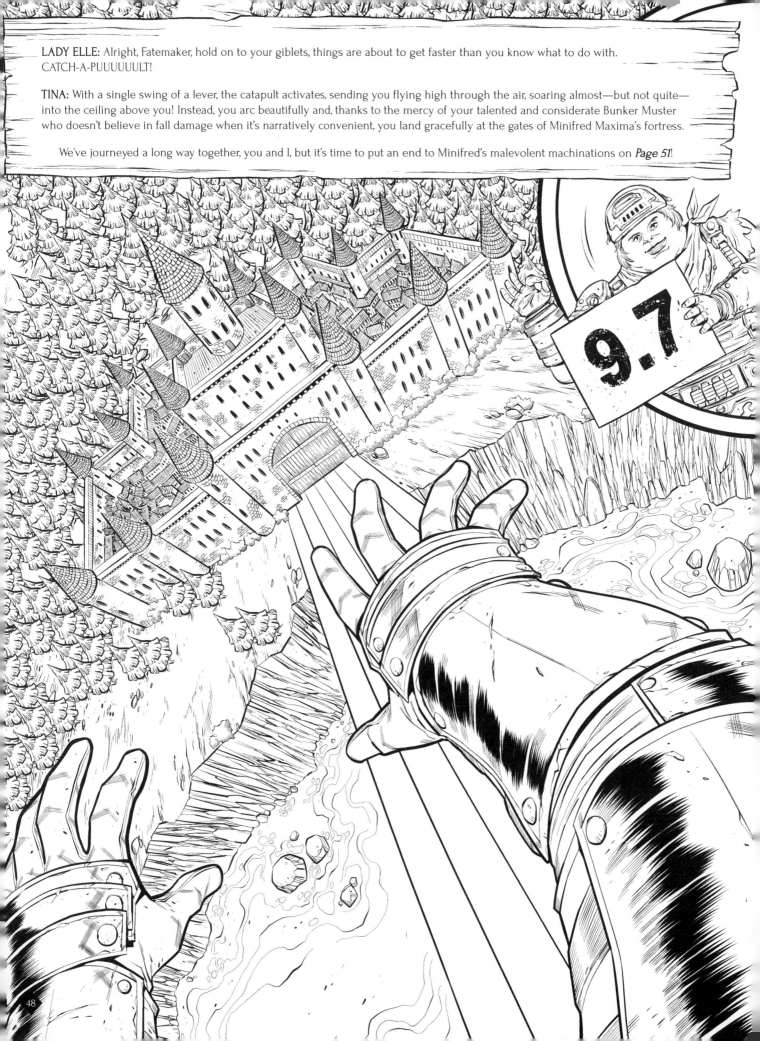

LADY ELLE: Alright, Fatemaker, hold on to your giblets, things are about to get faster than you know what to do with. CATCH-A-PUUUUUULT!

TINA: With a single swing of a lever, the catapult activates, sending you flying high through the air, soaring almost—but not quite—into the ceiling above you! Instead, you arc beautifully and, thanks to the mercy of your talented and considerate Bunker Muster who doesn't believe in fall damage when it's narratively convenient, you land gracefully at the gates of Minifred Maxima's fortress.

We've journeyed a long way together, you and I, but it's time to put an end to Minifred's malevolent machinations on *Page 51*!

LADY ELLE: Alright, Fatemaker, hold on to your giblets, things are about to get faster than you know what to do with. CATCH-A-PUUUUULT!

TINA: With a single swing of the lever, the catapult activates, and . . . oooh, hold on, I did not calibrate these numbers right. Math, amirite, heh heh . . . heh. Yeah, so, you arc through the air, uh, quite beautifully, but, um . . . you maybe kinda sorta sail right past Minifred's fortress and keep going until you . . . collide with the side of the table at bone-obliterating speeds.

VALENTINE: Alright, hold on, everyone, it's a fantasy world! Maybe we don't need our bones!

TINA: Nah, you really do.

Your journey's come to an end, Fatemaker, NO BONES about it. Heh . . . well, maybe you'll be able to laugh about it by the time you get back to *Page 1*.

TINA: A rainbow wave of minifigures carries you through the depths of the Table Below, their resplendent colors lighting all the mysteries of these dark lands as you travel.

FRETTE: Was that an actual, life-size ratch I just saw?

VALENTINE: Ooh, and a friendly lady with a catapult?

TINA: The wonders of the paths not taken call out to you, Fatemaker, but you've no time to consider them now! Plenty of stuff to look out for during a second playthrough, though, just sayin'. For now, the minifigs deliver you to the gates of Minifred's fortress. However, they can go no farther! This battle is yours and yours alone.

Steel yourself for the final battle with Minifred Maxima as you enter the fortress on *Page 51*!

TINA: This is it, Fatemaker! The long, twisting road of adventure and anarchy has brought you to the fortress of Minifred Maxima. As you reflect on your journey, you know that you're ready for whatever surprise is waiting for you on the other side of OH MY GOD, WHAT IS QUEEN BUTT STALLION DOING HERE?!

MINIFRED: Ah, hello there! Yes, the queen and I were just going over the terms of her abdication from the throne. We both agree a monarchy is a bit of an outdated concept in our new evil-free world. Once she's obsolete, I'm going to safely seal her away in this Vault.

TINA: No! NO! You do not mess with Queen Butt Stallion! Why does everyone always mess with Queen Butt Stallion?

MINIFRED: It's a very effective way of making you lose focus, you must admit.

TINA: Gah, enough! Why are you trying to ruin my game? WHO EVEN ARE YOU?!

Brace for that reveal, then turn to *Page 52* to find out WHO EVEN IS SHE?!

TANNIS: And another hello, everyone.

TINA: TANNIS? What are you doing here?!

TANNIS: Tina, you posted an invitation all over Sanctuary for people to join your new campaign, and I thought social interaction could make for an interesting experiment between all my more challenging work. Since you all didn't arrive on time—

TINA: It's cool to be several hours late, everyone knows that!

TANNIS: —I went ahead and started playing. With a bit of studying, it was easy to figure out the optimal way to complete all the challenges you'd put together. From there, well, it seemed only natural to solve the whole game.

TINA: You didn't solve anything, you ruined the game for everyone else! Agh, Fatemaker! You know what to do!

Alright, let's try this again! Charge Minifred and fight one-on-one on *Page 53*!

Make a roll of 10 or more to try a sneakier approach! Charge Minifred but slip behind her to *Page 54* at the last moment.

52

TINA: You charge right at Minifred, weapon in hand, and swing with all your might! THWACK!

MINIFRED: Hmm, was that supposed to hurt?

TINA: B-b-but all the training we did!

MINIFRED: Yes, good for you. But it's not like I was resting on my laurels, either. Here, let me show you with a THWACK of my own!

Ooh. Ooh, this is too graphic for the age range we're going for. Ooh, hard cut, hard cut! Look anywhere else! Like *Page 1* maybe!

TINA: You charge right at Minifred, weapon in hand, and . . . psych!

MINIFRED: What?!

TINA: The Fatemaker's only had, like, a couple dozen pages of training, there's no way they're a match for you. But they don't NEED to be because they have the key to your Vault! And we all know Vaults love to swallow up beings of immense power!

MINIFRED: Wait, no, hold on. I didn't plan for this! Stop it! Stop pulling me in, I say! I built you, Vault!

TINA: Fatemaker! Take it home!

Put Minifred under lock and key on *Page 55*!

Hold on! If you've found the eraser, the pen, and the errata sheets, maybe, just maybe . . . you can find another way on *Page 57*.

TINA: The Fatemaker may not be the strongest in the land, but with a decisive final kick, they're the hero the Wonderlands need! With one last cry, the overpowered, pesky, and all-around annoying Minifred Maxima is sealed away in the newly minted . . . Vault of the Min-Maxer!

FRETTE: Those adjectives seem a little harsh, Tina.

VALENTINE: Yeah, Tannis is still our friend! Well, as much as she's anyone's friend.

TINA: But . . . but she ruined the game! And there's no stopping the Vault now, so can we just see this thing through?

See how it all wraps up on *Page 56*.

TINA: So, uh, yeah, the Vault is sealed and . . . Minifred is gone forever.

TANNIS: I see. Well, I suppose this was a fun enough distraction while it lasted. I really should be getting back to the lab, then.

TINA: Ahem, yeah, thanks for . . . thanks for playing. Uh, good job, Fatemaker! You've saved the Wonderlands and now we can . . . can . . . agh, this felt a lot more satisfying when it was my own Player Character or dumb stupid Jack we were beating up!

VALENTINE: Well, this is . . . technically a good ending, right?

TINA: Sure, fine, yeah! Woo! Still . . . kind of a bummer. If only there had been a better way . . .

You've saved the Wonderlands, Fatemaker! If only everyone wasn't so bummed out about it. Well, maybe you can go back to *Page 1* and try to find a different solution.

TINA: Gah, I don't want to kick Tannis out of the game! She was clearly having fun, even if it wasn't MY idea of fun. But we've got to do something about Minifred, and . . . oh! As the Vault rages, you can sense the treasure already hiding within. That's right, it's Minifred's Character Sheet! With the items you've gathered on your journey—all clearly placed with great intention and foresight by your wise and wonderful Bunker Master—there may be a way to fix this whole mess yet! Grab that sheet and get to work, Fatemaker!

Reject the maximum and the minimum to find balance in the Bunker on *Page 58*!

The power of the Character Sheet . . . it calls to you. Give in to its siren song on *Page 60*.

TINA: Oh yeah, here we go! First, the eraser allows you to remove those broken abilities! With the pen, we can bring a more reasonable set of stats to the page permanently! And lastly, add that errata in, Fatemaker! That's the last bit of adjustment we need to make a character that's strong enough to face the Wonderlands but squishy enough to get completely flattened if enough rolls go wrong! Minifred Maxima, I declare thee . . . Balanced!

Bury the hatchet with Minifred and start a new adventure on *Page 59*.

TANNIS: Hmm, I see. Far from an optimized build, but still playable.

TINA: That's what I was going for, yeah. And . . . I get what you were going for, too. I want players who can come up with creative solutions to problems! Just maybe play when we're all together, y'know?

TANNIS: Hmm, I do suppose the social interaction aspect is why I wanted to play this game in the first place. Though she may no longer be as powerful, nothing can ever truly dull the sharp, analytical mind of Minifred Maxima. And now, she'll have an audience for her great deeds . . . and some friendly assistance when she can't handle it on her own.

TINA: Oh, she's for sure going to be challenged. Now that I've seen the sort of difficult problems you like, I can take my adventures to a whole new level.

TANNIS: Fatemaker! What do you say we team up and run some experiments on collaborative storytelling?

TINA: Ooh hoo hoo, I smell a new adventuring party taking shape. Well, give it all you've got, you two, because this Bunker's about to get a whole lot more Badass! Starting with the swarm of Badass enemies that have suddenly surrounded you! Hope you're ready for a fight, because you know what comes next!

    You sure do, Fatemaker! It's the start of a brand-new adventure, so it's time to roll for initiative!

TINA: Fatemaker? Fatemaker, I see you erasing Minifred's name, but not any of her broken stats. Uh, why are you tearing up the errata? Fatemaker, no! Don't write your name in pen!

FRETTE: Yeah, they are definitely not stopping!

TINA: You're really doing this?! Fine! As you write your name in and combine your old sheet with Minifred's, you feel a surge of unimaginable power course through your body! Just buttloads of the stuff! Immeasurable with broken, busted power is your now ascendant form. We've traded one broken Player Character for another, does that make you happy?

Go to *Page 61* to see just how happy it makes you!

TINA: Well, I'm glad YOU'RE happy, Fatemaker, because it's going to make this next part even more hilarious to me! As you relish in your newfound cosmic power, you find your body being pulled by an even greater force! That's right, dingus, that open Vault you clearly forgot about! It's still hungry for a broken Player Character, and since Minifred's no longer on the menu, you'll have to do! Oh, you fight it with everything you've got, but it's just not enough to stop you from getting swallowed up. THWAM goes the door, trapping you inside. And so ends the tale of our last-minute traitor, corrupted so by the promise of unlimited power. Their mistake? Forgetting that this is MY table. But hey, you've become the center of a new legend in the Wonderlands. Far and wide, they'll tell tales about the Vault of the Fatemaker. But it will never ever ever be opened again . . . EVER!

You're not the first adventurer whose desire for fat loot outweighed their common sense, Fatemaker. Consider this a learning experience as you head back to *Page 1*.

INSIGHT
EDITIONS

PO Box 3088
San Rafael, CA 94912
www.insighteditions.com
 Find us on Facebook: www.facebook.com/InsightEditions
 Follow us on Instagram: @insighteditions

Published by Insight Editions, San Rafael, California, in 2024.

ISBN: 979-8-88663-562-1

Publisher: Raoul Goff
VP, Co-Publisher: Vanessa Lopez
VP, Creative: Chrissy Kwasnik
VP, Manufacturing: Alix Nicholaeff
VP, Group Managing Editor: Vicki Jaeger
Publishing Director: Mike Degler
Art Director and Designer: Catherine San Juan
Editor: Sadie Lowry
Editorial Assistant: Jeff Chiarelli
Managing Editor: Maria Spano
Senior Production Editor: Nora Milman
Production Associate: Tiffani Patterson
Senior Production Manager, Subsidiary Rights: Lina s Palma-Temena

Text by Jordan Alsaqa
Illustrations by Elmer Damaso

Special Thanks to the team in Gearbox Licensing and 2K Games

ROOTS of PEACE   REPLANTED PAPER

Insight Editions, in association with Roots of Peace, will plant two trees for each tree used in the manufacturing of this book. Roots of Peace is an internationally renowned humanitarian organization dedicated to eradicating land mines worldwide and converting war-torn lands into productive farms.

Manufactured in China by Insight Editions

10 9 8 7 6 5 4 3 2 1